In the Land of Pele,

In the Land of the Extraordinary!

Kahu
Robert Kalama Frutos

One of Hawai'i's best known Camera Artist's
Internationally-known Author &
Long Time Big Island Resident

Text by Robert Frutos

ISBN-13: 978-1505668490   ePub ISBN-10: 1505668492

Also by Robert Frutos;

Hawai'i Sacred Sites of the Big Island Places of
Presence, Healing & Wisdom

Aloha Spirit: The True Essence of Hawaiian Spirituality

Aloha Spirituality A Bridge to Oneness
Living the Rainbow Path

Day Hikes in Hawai'i Volcanoes National Park: The
Best Places to See the Unusual, Find the Unexpected,
and Experience the Magnificent!

See full list of book titles by Robert Frutos on Page 98

See full list of book titles by Robert Frutos on Page 98

www.hawaiiphototours.org

www.hawaiisacredsitestours.com

www.robertfrutos.com

email: rfphoto3@gmail.com   Phone: 808 345 – 7179

Dedication

To Goddess Pele,
and those who find inspiration
and solace in Her Presence,

to those who are consciously striving
to bring a much needed balance
of Divine Feminine qualities into the world,

and to Priya,
who continually endeavors
to bring higher awareness and true aloha -
to all whose path she crosses,
she is an inspiration to all!

An Offering to Goddess Pele

Halema'uma'u Crater

All Images by Robert Frutos

Table of Context

Preface

Pele is well-known as the Hawaiian Goddess of Volcano and Fire. Her long-standing reputation of being a wrathful and destructive force - is the one *most* recognized and *always* emphasized from the western standpoint.

The Hawaiian perspective holds yet an entirely different relationship to the Goddess Pele, including - not only an ancestral kinship and common lineage, but a remarkable endearment, and an extraordinary spiritual inner connecttedness. One of deepest respect, alliance, and admiration.

From this approach, Pele is not merely a wrathful and destructive force, but rather a benevolent benefactor... a Living Goddess that is Present in now time, a protector; a friend who is loving, generous, encouraging, inspiring and supportive.

Pele plays many roles: Pele is the Goddess of the Volcano, Pele is the Goddess of the Fire, Pele is the Flame of Passion, Pele is the Fire of Purpose, Pele is the Goddess/Divine Mother. She is ultimately an expression of unconditional love, and the embodiment of the Divine Feminine.

While this is not a factual rendering of the Goddess Pele, nor even a historical account of her feats and achievements, it is rather a lyrical, expressive account centered on Her True Spiritual Gifts, from a Mu-Hawaiian perspective... drawn from the Mu-Hawaiian ancient oral tradition of song and chants.

7

This is also a wholehearted invitation to explore and discover Pele's deeper significance and magnificence, and the vital role she plays in the transformation of world today!

In Pele's Domain

E Pele e!
Ke akua o ka pohaku 'ena'ena,
'Eli e'li kau mai!

E Pele e!
O goddess of the burning stones,
Let awe possess me!

- Ancient Hawaiian Prayer

1

Pele: Hawaiian Goddess of the Volcano

Goddess Pele is well-known as the Hawaiian
Volcano and Fire Goddess. Aligned with volcanoes
Pele is implicitly associated with destruction and
violence.

Pele, known by many names is most widely known
as **Pele-honua-mea:** (Pe-lay-ho-new-a-may-a) **She
Who Shapes the Sacred Land.** In this role from a
Hawaiian perspective, her primary function is as a
regenerative and creative power.

The Goddess Pele holds the powerful energies
of both destruction and creation firmly in her hands
and Her long-standing reputation of being of a
wrathful and destructive force is the one *most*
recognized and *always* emphasized from a western
standpoint, the Kahuna of old (wisdom – keepers of
the Hawaiian traditions and culture) viewed Pele
as a dynamic creative force.

They talked of Her in terms of regeneration rather
than devastation, aligning Her with rejuvenate events
from the daily cycle of the wonder of life: the new
day, the rising sun, the northeast trade winds, rain
from the east.

From this approach, Goddess Pele's volcanoes are viewed more as a creative force. She creates and shapes the land, clearing away the old and laying the foundation for the new. In this light, the Goddess Pele as the Dynamic Creator… is ultimately an expression and the embodiment of Divine Creative Power. *She is the Energy of Dynamic Action.*

Pele as "**She who Shapes the Sacred Land**" can be seen as a Goddess Mother constantly birthing new land a continual process of dynamic and creative action: generating, recreating, and forging the landscape.

In doing so, Pele mirrors our own dynamic creative power - how we are constantly creating and shaping our own life with a constant flow of powerful energy that we project through our thoughts, our words, our feelings, our beliefs, and intentions, as well as our imagination.

In this way we can shape and create the very core and foundation of our deepest dreams and our highest aspirations, and ultimately create and manifest our own inspired life.

Pele offers many gifts towards creating and manifesting our highest aspirations, and one of the most powerful and profound gifts of the **Goddess Pele *is* Fire Power.**

Pele Birthing New Land

2

Pele: As the Goddess of Fire

Pele is the Flame of Passion, Pele is the Fire of Purpose *and* Pele is the Glowing Essence of Eternal and Profound Love.

She is an eternal spark of creation, and ultimately an expression of unconditional love, and the embodiment of the Divine Feminine.

The Fire Element brings Energy! The Element of Fire is a tremendous force for transmuting and clearing out old, and/or stagnate energy.

And when invoked - Pele can be called upon for physical energy, motivation, empowerment, and inner strength.

Pele, most aligned with the Fire Element, serves as a clear example *of our eternal connection to the Divine Flame.*

Pele will guide us to utilize our fire power wisely through honoring *our own inner flame.*

A Prayer to Pele

3

Pele: Goddess of Dynamic Divine Feminine Force

Pele demonstrates exquisite feminine beauty combined with unquestionable capability, steadfast strength, dignity, *and divine power.*

Goddess Pele also helps to clear the illusions that we are incapable, and helps us to realign with our Highest Potential so that we may realize our own Divine Truth.

She sets fire to the falsehood that women are craven and that to be feminine means to be fragile and passive, *providing a platform for both women and men - to transcend illusions related to feminine power.* Pele brings confidence, courage, and promotes dynamic positive action.

Upon our request through **pule**/prayer - Pele will assist us in rekindling our own inner fire - igniting our lives with more enthusiasm, passion, & purpose.

In this way, the Goddess Pele reminds us that we each have a gift to share in the world and will encourage us to acknowledge and express our unique talent.

She can help stimulate our creative energy and motivate us to fully experience life, ultimately as both meaningful and fulfilling.

Moreover, Pele is extremely protective and will help those who call on her to feel safe and secure, as well as empowered. She can be approached with deep reverence and respect as both *akua* (god) and *aumakua* (spiritual ancestor or ancestor god.)

Or, viewed as some see Her: Pele's form as the landscape itself. She can also be experienced through a deep sense of inner connectedness.

It is not uncommon that Hawaiians, as well as others who have come to the islands, have cultivated and nurtured an inner personal relationship with Her. Nor is it surprising that Pele is the most loved, feared, colorful, and famous goddess in all of Polynesia.

Once you begin to see through Her intense, passionate nature, you will begin to understand that it is not a wrathful essence at all, *but rather one of extraordinary transformation.*

Pele detests disrespect in any form, and especially to the earth, and to the Hawaiian native culture. And when offended (as known by Her reputation) Her retribution is sure and swift: immediately destroying and transforming, turning the flow of energy towards fairness and balance.

Goddess Pele comes with infinite and profound love, and is an awesome ally to those who desire to transcend the illusions of fear and limitation.

Pele is dedicated to our realizing our True Power: the Power of Divine Love. She is devoted to helping us realize and express our creative power in a way that brings benefit, blessings, and beauty to ALL.

Pele's Heart

Halema'uma'u Crater

4

In the Land of Pele
In the Land of the Extraordinary!

Part 1

In Pele's domain - the horizon stretches beyond the limits of imagination, and the terrain defies logic. Walking through the vast wild lands that surround Pele's dwelling, Halema'uma'u Crater, one is awe – struck by both the raw beauty and the massive devastation.

There are few places on the planet more mind-boggling: a tortured, buckled, and deformed topography of fresh barren lava that eventually gives birth to a parade of determined emerging life forms.

First appearing on a sea of barren lava is a myriad of lichen, in colors of grey, green, red and yellow.

Then along come the ferns, commonly known as the dotted polypody. Then the ama'u ferns slowly materialize, followed by the resilient and distinguished ohia trees imbued with Pele's favorite blossom - the brilliant deep red lehua flower. Following in due course are the beautiful and graceful koa forests.

New Ferns on Barren Lava

Lehua Blossom – Pele's Favorite Flower

In synergistic combination - they begin to create and
establish wholesome ecosystems that will regenerate
and replenish the land, as well as revealing the
vitality of the forceful dynamics of creation, and the
power and preciousness of all life.

The Preciousness of All Life

5

In the Land of Pele
In the Land of the Extraordinary!

Part 2

As you walk through these vast lands you will come
across evidence of ancient Hawaiian villages,
and their cultural way of life. You may perchance
upon powerful petroglyphs whose meaning to most
have been lost with the ages.

Petroglyphs,
Pu'u Loa Petroglyph Field

Petroglyph,
Pu'u Loa Petroglyph Field

You will find stonewalls built for many needs:
from wind protection to long ago settlements, from
ahu (shrines) to heiau (outdoor Hawaiian temples.)

You may find that these sites - considered sacred
sites by many allow you an insight or an experience
into another time and place or perhaps "speak to you"
in some way.

Simply allow yourself to receive whatever gift or
message is being offered and of course,
offer gratitude in return.

Through time, many of the old Hawaiian villages, heiau, and landmarks, have been damaged or destroyed by earthquakes and tsunamis, especially along the coast.

But there are still *many* places one can go to get a sense for what it was like to live in the profound beauty, harmony, and wonder of an ancient time... infused with the Power of Presence, and the Light of Spirit.

Sacred Ahu (Shrine) in a Sea of Lava

Ancient Ahu with Offerings

6

In the Land of Pele
In the Land of the Extraordinary!

Part 3

The land of Pele is indeed a magical place.
It is a land where the world of the visible and the
world of the invisible begin to mingle and merge.
Where the veils between reality and Spirit become
increasingly transparent.

Every pu'u (hill), every landscape, every unique
landmark, have a story to tell as real and tangible
as *your* own life story.

Those who take the time to really experience
the spirit of the land, may well be rewarded
in many and unexpected ways... instantaneous
insights, profound understandings, and/or an ever-
deepening awareness of a "presence" may reveal
themselves in a sudden and often unanticipated
manner.

It is as though the ancestors and Spirits *are waiting*
to share with you **that Spirit lives, that ALL life is
sacred, that you are embraced, loved and
protected - beyond your wildest imagination.**

And all you have to do to access this spiritual actualityis take the first step - all you have to do is *open yourself up to the possibility* of Divine awareness and presence.

The Hawaiian traditional viewpoint is that *everything* is created from the Divine Source.

That *everything* is made of **mana** which means universal divine spiritual power/spiritual energy. This life view created their spiritual foundation and understanding... that all life is a sacred gift from **ke Akua: Spirit.**

Therefore they lived/live accordingly, with reverence and *pono* (in balance) with one another and the natural world, and were intimately and intuitively aware of their surroundings and the blessings that sprang forth from them.

An Offering of Gratitude
Halem'uma'u Crater

7

In the Land of Pele
In the Land of the Extraordinary!

Part 4

In Hawai'i Volcanoes National Park means of entry to the wild lands and wilderness areas are via both convenient roadways and easily accessible hiking trails.

To get a real feel for, and an experience of, the vast panoramas and the spirit of the land, I highly encourage any number of hikes including: the Kā'u Desert/Footsteps Trail, Mauna Ulu Trail, Kilauea Iki Trail, Devastation Trail, and the Mauna Iki Trail.

There are miles and miles of open hiking trails many of them follow pre-existing ancient Hawaiian pathways. From the serene lush forests of ferns and flowering trees, across the extensive twisted and hardened lava flows, to the immense beauty of the Pacific ocean, these paths crisscross the land in a pattern of dramatic and eye - catching horizons that surpass ones' expectations.

Give yourself permission to take some time, and plan a hike... such as the one from the end of Hina Pali road to Halape, an old Hawaiian Village. Though decimated through the years by earthquakes and tsunamis it is one of the most beautiful remote locations in all of Hawaii for the rich beauty that abounds and the deep feeling of long ago Hawaii.

The first 2.2 miles are an amazing 1,400 ft. drop in elevation - from 2280 ft. to 880 ft., through seemingly unending switchbacks. Once on the flat, a high, large bluff between the *pali* (cliff) and the ocean... time begins to slow down and you realize you are now marching to the beat of different drum.

You are entering a world of timelessness where the only sounds you hear are the gentle lapping of the sea and a soft sweet breeze.

Here you are surrounded with vast horizons and unequaled raw beauty, where the ancestors welcome you and Pele's interaction with the landscape are oft times a stunning display, revealing Her dynamic and creative handywork while at the same time making an undeniable declaration of Her Presence.

Eventually the trail takes you around the shoulder of Pu'u Kapukapu. then down its flank, with unsurpassed ocean views.

From there Halape soon comes into full view – an oasis of gently swaying palms, with a welcoming white sand beach, and an energetic, cobalt colored sea, with the small but distinct Ke'a'oi island just off shore (a recognized bird sanctuary).

Spend some time here, *Experience* the beauty and wonder, *feel* the blessings, and *connect* with the ancestors.

Halape Sunrise
Looking East

Upon return to the trailhead you may choose to go back the same way you hiked in, climbing the 2,880 ft. from sea level including the 1,400 ft. elevation rise of those endless switch backs, or you may opt to take the 11 mile coastal trail that passes by Keauhou campground.

Halape with Rainbow Blessing
Looking West

Keauhou campground was once an old Hawaii fishing village, and also an important base of operations for a pulu business - the soft wool from the frond stalks of the fern tree, used for making bedding which was exported to the U.S., Canada, and Australia.

You can also choose to break the mileage in half by staying over night at Apua Point, another remote campground of rugged beauty - which is 6 miles from Halape. And finish up the last 5 miles the next day, venturing out and rejoining civilization at Chain of Craters Road.

If you have the time and energy you won't want to miss the Pu'u Loa Petroglyphs, only 0.7 miles further - the trailhead starts directly across the Chain of Craters Road from where the Halape trail ends.

The Kā'u Desert Trail

Or you may consider hiking the north - south Kā'u Desert Trail, potentially a 2 - 3 day backcountry hike. The Kā'u Desert Trail begins near the Halema'uma'u Crater. It is an old Hawaiian pathway that transverses the vast Kā'u Desert to the *pali* (cliff) overlooking

the vast Pacific. The first seven miles of the trail is currently closed, again, due to the Halema'uma'u Crater fume. (You needs catch this trail off the footprints trail – see page 50).

Puna Coast Trail
Nearing Chain of Craters Road

Petroglyph,
Near the Pu'u Loa Petroglyph Field

Out along the Kā'u Desert Trail

Along the way, you can choose to stay overnight at
the Pepeiao (hikers) cabin and then continue on
another 4.8 miles to Hina Pali Road where the trail
ends and Hina Pali Road begins.

Or you might decide to hike the whole trail in one day, as I did. This trail will take you through some pretty awesome and wide open country that will leave you in a state of awed admiration.

Kamakai'a Hill sign

It is open, and expansive, with the Kamakai'a hills (*pu'us*) off to the left (yours for the exploring) and hardened mind-blowing 1920 & 1974 lava flows to the left and right of you, till you arrive at the pali.

There you will find scattered forest with tall grasses and a to-die-for-view of the Pacific ocean.

As many times as I have hiked out there...
I have never seen (or even heard for that matter) another human being, while on this trail.
So if you like wide open spaces with BIG blue sky and a lot of elbow room (solitude) this may be a wise

choice of trail for you.

It is a 14 mile one way hike so be full prepared…
and it is always best on such long hikes to have at
least one hiking partner along, for your own safety
and company.

Access is through the Footprints Trailhead which
begins off of Highway 11 between mile marker 37
and mile marker 38.

Mauna Iki Trail

You may opt to experience the wild vastness of the
Mauna Iki trail, that cuts straight through the heart
of the Ka'u desert on an east-west route, also along
an ancient Hawaiian pathway. There you will find pit
craters with lava of phenomenal colors, red, bur-
gundy, orange, yellow - in an otherworldly terrain.

Pele's Hair

Pit Crater along the Mauna Iki Trail 2

This trail will take you through areas of grey/black sand dunes, across beige colored lava as well as steel blue patches of lava. All with expansive and seemingly endless horizons in all directions.

It will reveal what appears to be lengths of green hair, in fact it is hair, or rather, it is known as Pele's hair. The green colored hair-like texture made from the alchemy of lava eruptions, all born of the 1790 Halema'uma'u Crater explosion.

Standing out in this wild vastness one begins to realize our place in the full rhythm of life. Our overwhelming concerns and problems begin to lose their grasp on us, and as we begin to discover our innate sense of inner peace, and regain our inner sense of balance, gratitude naturally springs forth from the heart.

And we realize further we are not alone - that the ancestors/spirit guardians and *ke Akua:* Spirit are watching over us, protecting us, guiding us and embracing us.

And we are reminded of yet another dynamic and important aspect of the Hawaiian tradition: recognizing, honoring, and giving gratitude - to the ancestors and *akua*.

In the bigger picture within the Hawaiian cosmos it is understood that the ancestors are an integral part of both the past *and* the present.

Guardian Spirit

To stand anywhere, unaware of those who stood
before us… is to stand alone and isolated. To give

gratitude to those who have come before us,
reconnects us with the spirit of the ancestors,
and we more easily remember our deeper divine
connection with *ke Akua* : the Divine source.

Pit Crater along the Mauna Iki Trail
with Red, Burgundy, Orange, & Yellow Lava

It is in quiet moments such as these… when we stand
in full wonder and awe in the total magnificence
of creation, that our minds become calm and our
hearts open, and our awareness expands. And we
become aware of an undeniable and tangible
connection to the mystery of all life.

Looking out across the vast horizon of the landscape
and feeling an inner connectedness puts us in touch

with our deepest selves and reveals Pele the Goddess of Volcanoes and Fire, not merely to be a Goddess of unrelenting, mass destruction, and uncontrollable rage, only to be feared and dreaded, it displays another dimension and demeanor of Goddess Pele that few take the time to explore and discover.

The real possibility of another facet of Pele's personification - a dynamic creative power, an emissary of benevolent change, and all powerful Goddess of inspiring transformation.

Pele's Dynamic Creative Power

8

Pele: as a Symbol of Hope

My own relationship and experience with the
Goddess Pele is a combination, and sense of,
constant connectedness, inner communion,
and perpetual gratitude. I have clocked untold hours
in Her vast domain, day strolls, long hikes, overnight
camping in remote locations.

I am sometimes awe-struck, sometimes simply
stupefied by the unearthly and otherworldly tracts of
terrain that have been created by Pele's handiwork,
and then destroyed, and then recreated, and then
destroyed again.

One simply cannot help but wonder... how, within
this dry, windy, barren, mostly waterless devastation
how exactly ANYTHING can survive much less
continue to grow and then thrive.

Herein lies the lesson - by continually destroying
and regenerating, Pele reveals the very thin line
between life and death and just how truly precious
life is.

I have had many insights, revelations, and sacred
experiences, while transversing Pele's homeland.

In Pele's Otherwordly Domain

An insight I would like to share: is that while
roaming the twisted tormented landscapes,

I have seen with my own eyes - how even in the seemingly darkest hour, even while in the midst of vast devastation, completely barren ground and massive empty lava fields, that represent... and mirror back to us our own hardships and life struggles -

Hiking near Pele's Home

in these moments, when life itself seems barren and unforgiving and perhaps we feel stripped of all hope *that life does and will go on...*

and soon in the midst of the bareness and of the overwhelming devastation life forms begin to amass across the land, and all becomes regenerated

Emerging Ferns & Plant Life on Lava

and rejuvenated, and wholesome and eventually beautiful, and inspiring once again.

This is something to bear in mind, as we go through our most difficult moments in life. Through loss and unexpected change, and tragedy, even in the midst of hard pain, suffering, and grieving, (and believe me, I have had more than my fair share) once again a flow begins to take place that regenerates and rejuvenates and begins to seep into the depths of our hearts and souls, and brings us to that beautiful place of acceptance, inner peace and deeper understanding.

Returning us to our rightful place –
as being a source of love.

A Ray of Hope in Pele's Wonderland

9

In the Land of Pele
In the Land of the Extraordinary!

Part 5

Hiking out across the lava at 3:45 am is a challenge.
Leaving Volcano village at 2:30 am in order to begin
the hike at 3:45 am makes it all the more so.

Crossing the uneven, broken, and sometimes razor
sharp lava, adds another dimension of danger and
peril to an already precarious position. Almost
stepping upon a fresh lava flow, unexpectedly and
directly in front of you, takes equal parts - fear and
awesomeness to new levels.

Is it worth it you may be wondering? Ah yes,
absolutely... getting to a viewpoint where Pele
reveals Herself and unleashes her magnificent power
& beauty makes the journey not only worth it - but
turns it into a pilgrimage in every sense of the word.

Walking across the newest lava flows on the island
(and often, in the world) is in itself awe-inspiring.
Patterns, colors, shapes and textures exist in
unimaginable formations, configurations and
contours (which one can only see to fully
appreciate on the hike in daylight.)

Emerging Lava on a New Lava Flow

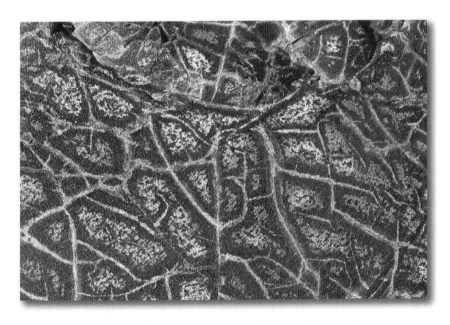

Pele's Lava Texture/Handiwork

Lava into Sea

Goddess Pele's artistry and handiwork in every direction are clearly and supremely present. But only when you get to the actual lava flow itself - does your connection unfold and unite into sheer wonder and delight.

Moreover, you see before your very eyes...
Pele at work (or is it Her play?) And this experience can take you deep inside yourself, and if you open yourself up enough - you can feel Her "inner" presence as well as, Her all loving embrace encircle you.

Sometimes you can just feel Her calling, and then it's off to the lava flows again. Ready to hike, I began at

4 am, full moon lighting up the sky and reflecting on the lava - the moon so bright never once was a flashlight used.

Three long miles one way across the lava plains. Almost there, crossing a " hot spot." This is where the lava is flowing in a lava tube directly under you. All of a sudden you notice that the cracks in the lava beneath your feet are bright red, alive, and glowing.

The air temperature and the earth temperature instantaneously heat up and if you stand in one place too long the soles of your footwear begin to smoke, and if you stand there longer than your instincts tell you is safe - the soles of your shoes begin to melt.

CRAZY TO DO IT?

Perhaps, but you learn to have a sense for what's truly safe, and what is not. I simply trust my intuition and place one foot carefully in front of the other, until I reach an unimaginable viewpoint, that is utterly awe-inspiring - way beyond words, or thoughts, or even a context in which to express them fully.

Witnessing the birthing of new land, which has been going on in Hawai'i for many millions of years. The interplay of fire and water - opposites working together in chaotic unison, to create land mass after land mass, island after island.

Cascading Fresh Lava

Lava into Sea 2

It's mesmerizing and powerfully irresistible, and puts things into a new and broad perspective, creating a sense of both timelessness and an ever - expanding awareness, where one can most easily feel and understand one's place in the flow of life.

Where one can gain a senseof inner clarity and new purpose,as all the little things, or seemingly big things, evaporate before this profound experience and visual magnificence.

On our return trip, crossing the "hot spot" a little closer to the coastline, the surface lava emerged, and we realized the lava we had just walked across was only a few minutes old.

With gratitude, we stayed a while longer and observed the many shapes, and forms, and textures, the lava creates as it moves down the coastal pali (cliff) and into the sea. Walking back to the car we were greeted by my old friend the rainbow, in full arc.

Once again, we offered gratitude to the beauty, power and Presence of Pele, and the sense that this could well have been the feeling and the experience of the very first dawn of all creation.

Rainbow on New Lava

10

In the Land of Pele
In the Land of the Extraordinary!

Part 6

Offerings for Pele

There is one area, that remains easily accessible, that was/is used by modern Kahuna as well as Kahuna of old. It is a place where prayers and offerings have been made to the Goddess Pele for many millennium.

The area is known as Uwēkahuna and translates as the "wailing Kahuna,"as in, wailing or crying or

Prayers to Pele

calling – for guidance or a vision.

This area is very powerful, and if you are inwardly still enough, your awareness will expand to include an undeniable and commanding Presence.

To be embraced in this awareness is to be aligned with the very source of creation itself – Pele's all pervading, profound, and permeating Presence.

In this location - once stood a heiau (Hawaiian Outdoor Temple) in honor of Pele, and endless ceremonies were performed here, in gratitude and reverence.

There was once a trail that ran down to the very edge

of Halemaʻumaʻu crater from the heiau, as those worshipping Pele would often leave gifts and offering on the edge of Halemaʻumaʻu Crater.

Still today, ceremonies are held and offerings are left in Pele's honor, and you will see them scattered randomly at the caldera's edge.

Ceremony to Pele at the Caldera's Edge

For a more quiet experience (compared to Jaggar Museam) go to the Kīlauea Overlook – still a part of the Uwēkahuna Bluff. From there you gain a different and unique perspective of Pele's handiwork.

You can further venture along the caldera's edge,

following the asphalt trail for more vantage points.

There was another heiau a couple of blocks to the left of the actual Kīluaea Overlook. All that's left today is a single stone, in place between the asphalt path and the caldera's edge.

The View From Kīluaea Overlook

There is *much* power and energy in this Kīluaea summit area, home of Pele - the Goddess of Volcanoes and of Fire.

Pele's Blush at Twilight

The best times to be there are sunrise and especially twilight, as day gives birth to night. This is the time Pele, in Her pluming form will start to blush, and the darker it gets, She becomes the most colorful, and therefore the most radiant and beautiful.

(Directions to this area on page 87.)

Pele's Glow & Full Moon

11

Pele: as the Goddess/Divine Mother

Throughout the world there is a deep reverence
and worship of the Divine Mother, who has appeared
in many forms right through history.

The Divine Mother/Goddess/Divine Feminine
is the powerful, creative and loving force of the
universe. Pele is an expression of this force.

Most of the indigenous peoples of the world,
throughout history - have been fully aware of this
expression of the divine, and have honored and
worshipped the Mother aspect - across endless time.

Hawaiian Spirituality, for the whole of time
has not only worshipped the supreme Creator Keawe
also known as 'Io, but also His female counterpart,
Goddess Uli, a manifestation of the Divine Mother.
(Uli is her abbreviated name, which means blue.
Her full name means "the spiritual breast of heaven
from whom the milk of life flows.")

Hawaiian culture, as well as all indigenous cultures
were keenly aware that ALL of life's gifts *were born
of the Mother* - the Mother Earth, the Human Mother,
the Goddess Mother, the Divine Mother.

The Mother is the bearer of ALL life and without the Mother or the feminine reality, life would quite simply cease to exist.

The qualities of the Mother - unconditional love, tenderness, receptivity, patience, sensitivity, humility, intuitive awareness, and open heartedness, are all qualities greatly lacking in todays world.

Divine Mother and Her pantheon of Goddesses - constantly remind us and reawaken us to this urgent and necessary need for balance between the Divine Feminineand the Divine Masculine.

Pele offers many gifts towards creating and harmonizing this balance, and one of the most powerful and profound gifts of the Goddess Pele is: the gift of absolute love, Divine love above ALL.

Pele's Heart

Directions to Uwēkahuna

Uwēkahuna Bluff is located at the Halema'uma'u Crater Overlook (they are one and the same) at the Jaggar Museum in Hawai'i Volcanoes National Park.

Once you reach the overlook, you will be peering into Volcano Goddess Pele's home and sanctuary. Although her flows are plunging into the ocean, or elsewhere, to the Hawaiian people her principle residence is in Halema'uma'u Crater.

Directly tied into Hawaiian tradition and history, are the many unending stories, legends and myths of the Goddess Pele.

Irrevocably a part of the culture, She is one of the most active Goddesses in Hawai'i today, clearly the one most powerfully present.

So entwined is Her energy and vitality in the Hawaiian consciousness, that She is a living, thriving, dynamic force – one to call upon in times of need, one to respect at all costs, and one to venerate and worship.

So a visit to Halema'uma'u Crater, where Pele reveals Herself and unleashes her magnificent power & beauty makes the journey not only worthwhile - but Her Presence clearly and supremely present.

From the Halema'uma'u Crater Overlook perch, Goddess Pele's artistry and handiwork can be seen in every direction.

To Get to the Halema'uma'u Crater Overlook

Hawai'i Volcanoes National Park is 29 miles from Hilo on Highway 11 between mm 28 & 29. If you're staying in Kailua-Kona, it's 100 miles, or about a 2 and a half hour drive to the park.

Admission is $10 per vehicle. Once you pay the fee, you can come and go as often as you want for 7 days. Hikers and bicyclists pay $5; bikes are allowed only on roads and paved trails.

From the entrance gate proceed straight forward.

You will shortly pass the Visitors Center on the right hand side (about a block) a good place for information, restrooms, and free compelling films about actual lava flows in the park and elsewhere on the Big Island.

On the left, across from the Visitors Center, is Volcano House - a historic old hotel on the crater's rim. A good place for a meal, or a snack. The hotel has an excellent gift shop and fabulous views of the crater.

Continuing on from the visitor center, you will soon

come to the Steam Vent area (definitely worth a visit) and then you will continue past the Kilauea Military Camp (also known as KMC) which will be on your right hand side. Here you find a store, a cafeteria, and a gas station. However, you must be active or retired military personnel to use these facilities.

Continue on another 1.4 miles to the Jaggar Museum Parking lot. Park here and walk over to the Jaggar Museum. It is another excellent place for information regarding all things lava (the museum includes a gift shop, drinking water and restrooms.)

The Halema'uma'u Crater Overlook is at the far end of the museum. You can't miss it, its where a number of placards are - that describe the craters history, and has a-view-to-die-for (as they say.)

Right here where the overlook is - *is* Uwēkahuna Bluff. Uwēkahuna Bluff extends down and past the Kilauea Overlook - a half mile down an asphalt trail you can connect with at the northern edge of the Jaggar Museum parking lot. There is a trail marker there that is easily found.

You can also gain access to the Kilauea Overlook and parking lot, by driving about a 1/2 mile back down the road away from the Jaggar Museum parking lot (back the way you originally came.)

You will see a sign that says Kilauea on the right, and you will be turning left. Follow the road to the parking lot and there you will find a paved trail to the overlook.

Visitor Centers & Information

Contact info: Hawai'i Volcanoes National Park, P.O. Box 52, Hawaii National Park, HI 96718 www.nps.gov/havo, 808/985-6000).

The Kīlauea Visitor Center is at the entrance to the park, just off Hwy. 11. It is open daily from 7:45 am to 5 pm.

Eruption Updates

Everything you want or need to know about Hawai'i's volcanoes, from what's going on with the current eruptions to where the next eruption is likely to be, is now available on the Hawaiian Volcano Observatory's new website, http://volcanoes.usgs.gov/hvo/activity/kilaueastatus.php.

The site is divided into areas on Kīlauea (the currently erupting volcano), Mauna Loa (which last erupted in 1984), and Hawai'i's other volcanoes. Each section provides photos, maps, eruption summaries, and historical information.

You can also get the latest on volcanic activity in the park by calling the park's 24-hour hot line -

(808) 985-6000

Double Rainbow in Pele's Playground

About the Author:
Kahu Robert Kalama Frutos

Kahu Kalama is a wisdom-keeper of Mu - Hawaiian spirituality, as well as, of Hawai'i's sacred sites.

Kahu Kalama is also a spiritual intuitive, healer, visionary artist, esoteric (soul) astrologer, internationally recognized author/camera artist, and a Light Carrier of Aloha.

Tutored and mentored throughout the years, Kahu has trained with many of the Big Island Native Hawaiian cultural luminaries... Kumu (teachers) Kapuna (elders) and Kahuna. Kahu has been hanaied (adopted) into the spiritual & Hawaiian family of High Priestess Kahuna Kalei'iliahi.

Kahu has been trained in Hawaiian healing practices and given special permission to share Hawaiian spirituality, healing, & the mana of sacred sites by Kahuna Papa K. Kahu has been encouraged and blessed to share the ancient Universal Hawaiian and Lumerian truths by Kumu Kahuna Nui Ehulani

Kahu Kalama is also the founder of the Light of Aloha Foundation and Ministry, a not for profit educational venue for sharing inspiration, and techniques towards practical spiritual living.

Kahu has created a unique body of work woven together from a broad spectrum of training and varied experience - a spiritual educator, internationally recognized author, counselor, professional camera artist, a successful multi - business owner, photo tour guide, sacred site tour guide, healing practitioner and presenter.

Kahu offers support, encouragement, comfort, and assistance through mentoring, intuitive counseling, and spiritual coaching - allowing you a fresh perspective (a view of the large picture) a clear sense of direction, and greater inner alignment.

Kahu possesses a great depth and passion - that inspires you to realize that the spiritual world is not only possible and within our reach, but is an integral part of the fabric and fiber of our everyday reality.

Kahu offers tours, classes, workshops, retreats, and private consultations. He has authored many books - including *Hawai'i Sacred Sites of the Big Island Places of Wisdom Healing and Presence, Aloha Spirit: The True Essence of Hawaiian Spirituality and Aloha Spirituality A Bridge to Oneness Living the Rainbow Path*

His accomplishments provide insight into his

passion, enthusiasm, and creativity. Kahu is a gifted teacher/speaker with a unique ability to easily share and communicate "how to live" spiritual living skills.

He also brings the same passion – into sharing the Spirit of Aloha, and the beauty, wonder, and magnificence of the Hawaiian Islands.

You can reach Kahu Kalama at:

www.hawaiisacredsitestours.com

www.hawaiiphototours.org

www.robertfrutos.com

email: rfphoto3@gmail.com

Phone: 808 345 – 7179

Other Books by

Kahu Robert Kalama Frutos

aka Robert Frutos

Clarity, Inspiration, & Optimum Potential: A Concise Guide for Creating Infinite Possibility in YOUR Life!

In the Pursuit of Excellence: A Concise Guide for Creating Unlimited Possibility in YOUR Life, Business and/or Organization!

Photographing Nature in Hawaii: Capturing the Beauty & Spirit of the Islands,

Hawai'i Inspiration Aflame: A Passion for the Magnificence,

Hawaii How to Capture the Dynamic Islandscape: A Photographers Approach,

A Photographer's Guide to Hawai'i Volcanoes National Park: Being in the Right Place, at the Right time, for the Best Image

Day Hikes in Hawai'i Volcanoes National Park: The Best Places to See the Unusual, Find the Unexpected, and Experience the Magnificent!

With Beauty All Around Me: Inspirations to Touch the Heart, Heal and Uplift the Spirit

Walking in Beauty: Inspirational Seed Thoughts for Creating YOUR Best Life Possible

With Beauty All Around Me: Black & White Edition Inspirations to Touch the Heart, Heal and Uplift the Spirit

Hawai'i The Most Beautiful Places to Visit on the Big Island

Hawai'i The Best Beaches on the Big Island including the Best Snorkeling Locations

for more information about these books, go to:

http://rfphoto3.wix.com/booksbyrobert

or

www.hawaiisacredsitestours.com

Click on Robert's Links/Books

Lastly, I have one more photography book available, an inspiring coffee table book entitled: **Hawaii Inspiration Aflame: A Passion for the Magnificence**,

This is a rare book - one conceived, created, written, and photographed by a visionary artist with a unique and extraordinary vision. It is both an inspired celebration of the wonder and beauty of Hawai'i and an inspiring journey of discovery.

It's purpose is simple: to ignite your inspiration and reawaken your passion. Your Journey awaits you...

"Nature photographer, Robert Frutos, offers a unique vision. With sensitivity and awareness he draws from the world around him and communicates through his photographs a world of clarity, beauty, and wonder - through his extraordinary vision, inspiration, and a palette of light that both uplifts and inspires."

- J Donald Walters, world renown lecturer, author , artist
This book is only available directly from the author.
Email rfphoto3@gmail.com, or call 808 345-7179,
for more info./to obtain a copy.

**30 Pages Hardback Only Cost $65.00 plus &6.00
s&h**

An Offering to Pele

Made in the USA
Charleston, SC
04 January 2017